What's in Your Fast Food?

WHAT'S IN YOUR HOT DOG?

Jaclyn Sullivan

PowerKiDS press™

New York

To Nicole, the hot dog's number-one fan

Published in 2012 by The Rosen Publishing Group, Inc.
29 East 21st Street, New York, NY 10010

First Edition

Editor: Sara Antill
Book Design: Greg Tucker

3 1559 00232 7839

Photo Credits: Cover, pp. 4, 7 (bottom), 8, 9 (top), 11, 15 (bottom), 16 Shutterstock.com; p. 5 Digital Vision/Thinkstock; p. 6 George Heyer/Three Lions/Getty Images; p. 7 (top) © www.iStockphoto.com/eliandric; p. 9 (bottom) © www.iStockphoto.com/Wilson Valentin; p. 10 Hemera/Thinkstock; pp. 12, 14, 21 iStockphoto/Thinkstock; p. 13 Design Pics/Stock Foundry/Valueline/Thinkstock; p. 15 (top) D. Anschultz/Digital Vision/Thinkstock; pp. 17, 18 Creatas Images/Creatas/Thinkstock; p. 19 Yellow Dog Productions/The Image Bank/Getty Images; p. 22 Jupiterimages/Brand X Pictures/Thinkstock.

Library of Congress Cataloging-in-Publication Data

Sullivan, Jaclyn.
 What's in your hot dog? / by Jaclyn Sullivan. — 1st ed.
    p. cm. — (What's in your fast food)
 Includes index.
 ISBN 978-1-4488-6213-9 (library binding) — ISBN 978-1-4488-6385-3 (pbk.) —
ISBN 978-1-4488-6386-0 (6-pack)
 1. Frankfurters—Juvenile literature. 2. Sausages—Juvenile literature. 3. Meat—Health aspects—Juvenile literature. I. Title.
 TX749.S827 2012
 641.6'6—dc23

                              2011032102

Manufactured in the United States of America

CPSIA Compliance Information: Batch #WW12PK: For Further Information contact Rosen Publishing, New York, New York at 1-800-237-9932

Contents

All About Hot Dogs!

You can probably look at many foods you eat and guess what they are made of. Have you ever wondered, though, what is inside a hot dog? The answer will be different depending on what kind of hot dog you are eating!

Many people like the taste of hot dogs. Does it really matter, then, what they are made of? No matter how they taste, some foods are

Food gives our bodies the energy we need to be active. These boys are using energy playing basketball.

These kids are eating hot dogs topped with ketchup and mustard.

better for our bodies than others. Different foods give our bodies the different **nutrients** we need to stay healthy. Learning what is in hot dogs can help you decide if eating them is a healthy choice for you.

German Beginnings

Sausages have been eaten for hundreds of years in Europe. It is likely that the idea of eating sausages on bread rolls or buns came to the United States with German **immigrants** in the 1800s. In 1871, a German immigrant named Charles Feltman began selling sausages in buns at his restaurant in Coney Island, a part of Brooklyn, New York. By the 1890s,

Nathan Handwerker worked at Charles Feltman's Coney Island restaurant. In 1916, he opened Nathan's Famous, seen here in 1955. Nathan's Famous is now a fast-food chain with restaurants all across the United States.

people were calling a sausage eaten in a bun a hot dog.

Today, you can find hot dogs at sports games, fairs, restaurants, and movie theaters. Some people even sell hot dogs from street carts.

This hot dog cart is in New York City.

FAST-FOOD FACTS

Hot dogs are sometimes called franks after the city of Frankfurt, Germany, seen here. They are also called wieners after Wien, the German name for the city of Vienna, Austria.

7

Hot Dog Meats

Not all hot dogs are made of the same things. Some are made from beef and some from pork. Others are made from a mix of the two. Beef is what we call meat from cows. Pork is the meat of a pig.

Some hot dogs also have chicken and turkey in them. If chicken or turkey parts are used, they are

Pork comes from pigs. Bacon and ham also come from pigs.

often **mechanically separated**. This means that machines mash up different parts of the animals and push them through a strainer to take out the bones. Hot dogs can include the hearts, kidneys, and livers of chickens and turkeys, too. These parts are called **by-products**.

When a package of hot dogs says that they are all beef, that means that no other meats were used. The hot dogs still have many other ingredients, though.

FAST-FOOD FACTS

Products

Hebrew NATIONAL
MADE WITH PREMIUM CUTS of 100% KOSHER BEEF
QUARTER POUND BEEF FRANKS

Kosher hot dogs are usually made with only beef. The word "kosher" comes from Hebrew and means "fit to eat according to Jewish law." Pork is never used because it is not kosher.

Cooking and Casings

These hot dogs are hanging on a rack. Next they will be sprayed with liquid smoke for flavor and moved into an oven to cook.

To form a hot dog, the meat is chopped and mixed with spices and other **ingredients**, or parts, to form a paste. The paste is then squeezed into tubes called **casings**. The first casings used were made from the **intestines** of animals. Today, these are called natural casings. **Artificial** casings are made from plant or animal fibers. Once they are in their casings, hot dogs are cooked. Natural casings are left on

the cooked hot dogs. Artificial casings are usually taken off the hot dogs before they are packaged. Because these hot dogs have no casings when you eat them, they are called skinless!

Many natural casings are made from the intestines of sheep.

Hot Dog Buns

To make flour, wheat, seen here, is ground into a fine powder.

Hot dog buns are long and narrow so hot dogs fit nicely inside. Like all kinds of bread, hot dog buns are made with flour. Flour comes from a type of grass called wheat. To make a bun, flour is mixed with water, eggs, and a living thing that helps bread rise called yeast. Sugar and salt are often added, too. The flour mixture, called dough, is then rolled into finger-like shapes and baked.

You may have seen hot dog buns that have seeds on the outside. People sometimes bake pale yellow seeds called sesame seeds into buns. The smaller, dark seeds used are called poppy seeds.

Hot dog buns let you eat hot dogs without a knife or a fork. This makes them an easy food to eat outdoors!

What's on Top?

Many people like to put toppings on their hot dogs. These toppings are called **condiments**. Ketchup and mustard are common condiments. Another popular hot dog topping is pickle relish, which is made with cucumbers soaked in vinegar or salty water called brine.

Different toppings are popular in different parts of the United States. In California and Arizona, you might find hot dogs wrapped in bacon. New York City is known for

Different condiments add different flavors to hot dogs. These five hot dogs all have different toppings. The one in the middle is topped with spicy jalapeño peppers.

hot dogs topped with yellow mustard and an onion and tomato sauce. A Kansas City hot dog, popular in Kansas and Missouri, is topped with pickled cabbage, or sauerkraut, and swiss cheese.

This boy is eating a hot dog topped with chili. Hot dogs topped with chili are often called chili dogs.

FAST-FOOD FACTS

Michigan dogs are a type of chili dog that is popular in New York. Coney Island dogs, also topped with chili and named after the neighborhood in New York, are popular in Michigan!

Preservatives

Hot dogs and some other types of sausages can keep on a grocery store shelf for several weeks.

Once they are packaged, hot dogs can last for a few weeks or more. This is because they have **preservatives** in them. Preservatives keep food from spoiling, or going bad. Hot dogs often have preservatives in them called **nitrates**. Nitrates also help hot dogs keep their pink color.

Some studies have shown that nitrates cause an illness called cancer in lab mice. Hot dogs have fewer nitrates in them than the amounts that made the mice sick. However, many doctors think that kids should eat fewer nitrates in case they make people sick, too. At the grocery store, look for hot dogs made without nitrates.

Hot dogs are a popular food for campouts. They can be heated in a campfire, the way these people are doing.

17

Hidden Dangers

Instead of eating your hot dog with french fries or fried onion rings, try some fruit or vegetables.

Hot dogs often have a lot of salt added to them. Salt gives hot dogs some of their flavor. It also acts as a preservative. Salt helps nutrients move between different parts of our bodies. However, too much salt can hurt your kidneys and make your heart work harder to move blood around your body.

Hot dogs are often eaten for lunch at school. Try to pick healthy toppings for your hot dog. Adding vegetables to your plate will help you get the nutrients you need for the day.

Eating too much fat can also hurt your heart. The kinds of meats used in hot dogs have fat in them. Hot dog buns and toppings like chili and cheese can add even more fat.

Nutrition Facts

Serving Size 1 Hot Dog (49g)
Servings Per Container: 10

Amount Per Serving

Calories 150   Calories from Fat 130

	% Daily Value *
Total Fat 14g	22%
Saturated Fat 6g	30%
Trans Fat 0g	
Cholesterol 25mg	8%
Sodium 746mg	30%
Potassium 700 mg	20%
Total Carbohydrate 1g	0%
Dietary Fiber 0g	0%
Sugar 2g	
Protein 6g	12%

Vitamin A 0%	•	Vitamin C 0%
Calcium 0%	•	Iron 4%

*Percent Daily Values are based on a 2,000 calorie diet. Your daily values may be higher or lower depending on your calorie needs.

	Calories	2,000	2,500
Total Fat	Less than	65g	80g
Sat Fat	Less than	20g	25g
Cholesterol	Less than	300mg	300mg
Sodium	Less than	300mg	300mg
Total Carbohydrate		300g	375g
Dietary Fiber		25g	30g

Calories per gram:
Fat 9   •   Carbohydrate 4   •   Protein 4

Knowing how to read a label can help you decide if a food is healthy for you. Labels on hot dog packages tell you how much of each nutrient is in your hot dog. They also tell you how many **calories** are in your hot dog. Calories are a measure of the energy in our food.

This is an example of a label on a package of hot dogs. If you eat your hot dog in a bun or with any toppings, you will need to look at the labels on those packages to find the total amounts of calories and nutrients in your meal.

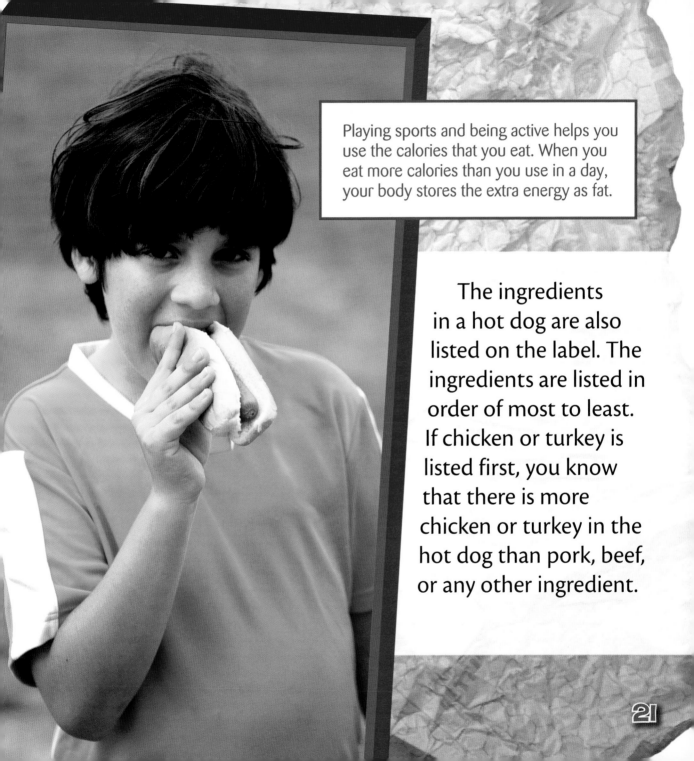

Playing sports and being active helps you use the calories that you eat. When you eat more calories than you use in a day, your body stores the extra energy as fat.

The ingredients in a hot dog are also listed on the label. The ingredients are listed in order of most to least. If chicken or turkey is listed first, you know that there is more chicken or turkey in the hot dog than pork, beef, or any other ingredient.

Healthier Hot Dogs

When you choose to eat healthy food, you are doing something good for your body.

Hot dogs can be eaten as part of a healthy diet. Even though they taste good, it is a good idea to eat them only once in a while. When you do eat hot dogs, try to choose kinds that have fewer preservatives and artificial ingredients.

You can also choose toppings, such as vegetables, that have more nutrients and less fat. Chicago hot dogs, topped with tomatoes, onions, pickles, and peppers, are a tasty choice!

Glossary

artificial (ar-tih-FIH-shul) Made by people, not nature.

by-products (BY-prah-dukts) The parts of an animal that are not generally eaten, including organs.

calories (KA-luh-reez) Amounts of food that the body uses to keep working.

casings (KAY-singz) Thin tubes that hold the ingredients of a hot dog together in a certain shape.

condiments (KON-duh-ments) Seasonings or sauces added to a food to give it flavor.

immigrants (IH-muh-grunts) People who move to a new country from another country.

ingredients (in-GREE-dee-unts) The different things that go into food.

intestines (in-TES-tinz) Parts of the digestive system that are below the stomach.

mechanically separated (mih-KA-nih-kuh-lee SEH-puh-rayt-ed) Relating to a process in which machines push pieces of meat through a strainer. This separates the bones from the meat that can be eaten.

nitrates (NY-trayts) Types of preservatives used in hot dogs and other processed meats.

nutrients (NOO-tree-ents) Food that a living thing needs to live and grow.

preservatives (prih-ZER-vuh-tivz) Substances that keep something from going bad.

Index

Web Sites

Due to the changing nature of Internet links, PowerKids Press has developed an online list of Web sites related to the subject of this book. This site is updated regularly. Please use this link to access the list:

www.powerkidslinks.com/food/dog/